BE CALM

Take a deep breath. How calm do you feel?

When life is weighing you down and it's all getting a bit much, you can begin to get a panicky feeling. This is your brain sending out stress signals, and it can affect all sorts of things – your ability to remember stuff, how well you can concentrate and even make you angry or sad.

That's why we, the editors of *Teen Breathe*, decided to put together this book. Every month we read dozens of articles about the obstacles that young adults face, and we've learned there are lots of things you can do to overcome them. Now we're excited to pass that knowledge on to you.

So next time the pressure builds up and you start to feel overwhelmed, why not pick up this book and take a moment? Use what's written inside to think about how you're feeling, why that might be and what you can do to help it subside.

Different people deal with stress in different ways. We hope that by finding your own unique way, you can give yourself the chance to shine, and be all that you were born to be.

KEEP CALM AND BELIEVE

CONTENTS

HOW CALM DO YOU FEEL?

Being a teen is stressful. Your parents demanding you act responsibly, pressure to do well at school and in exams, family and friendship dramas, hormones going crazy – no wonder it can sometimes feel overwhelming. You can't avoid all the stress in your life, but if you can recognise what gets you worked up, then you can learn how to handle it.

LET'S TALK ABOUT STRESS

1 What is stress?

Sometimes everything feels too much. Your parents want you to do things. Your school puts pressure on you. You want to keep up with friends. You feel… stressed.

When life is throwing a lot at you, your brain receives stress signals and you can start to get a panicky feeling. This can happen at any time, but it's usually because a situation or event is making you feel out of control, or you've been put under pressure to do something that you find hard.

2 Does everybody feel stressed?

Feeling stressed often comes when things change – right now, it might seem that everything is changing as you drift between childhood and adulthood. Sometimes you wish you were small (and maybe safe) again, sometimes you feel strong and grown up.

Your body is changing. People start asking more of you. Your feelings get more intense and can be difficult to express or control. You start discovering who you are – and who you'd like to become. None of this is easy. So, no wonder you're encountering new levels of stress in your life. You're not alone.

3 So some stress is natural then?

It's *very* natural to experience some stress when you face new challenges – as you stretch yourself to take on more responsibility or try new things. Feeling stressed for a short period of time can even help by making you feel more alert and propelling you to take action. Remember, the brain actually likes solving problems.

Everyone has different thresholds for stress. You may be able to cope with more stress than a friend, for example, but less than someone older than you. The good news is that no matter your current level, you can learn how to handle stress better.

Learning to face stress and deal with it will make you more resilient and less frightened. You'll discover an innate strength and courage to be proud of.

HOW DO I KNOW IF I'M STRESSED?

Stress shows itself in different ways – both emotionally and physically. *Here are some signs that you might be feeling stressed*:

* Lack of focus.

* Disturbed sleep, constantly tired.

* Lots of worrying.

* Snappier or more tearful than usual.

* More withdrawn.

* Feeling lonely and alone (with no one to talk to).

* Feeling down on yourself.

* Eating more or less than usual.

* Not able to disconnect from social media.

* Panicky or having panic attacks.

* More controlling or obsessive.

* Disconnecting from feelings, numbness.

Remember that some of these things can also be a natural part of being a teenager, so use your gut instinct.

'WORRYING DOESN'T TAKE AWAY TOMORROW'S TROUBLE. IT TAKES AWAY TODAY'S PEACE'

Randy Armstrong

SIX WAYS TO KEEP CALM

Different people have different methods of calming down when they're stressed. *Here are some techniques you could try. Which one works for you?*

1 Speak out

The first thing to do is to tune into, and then voice, how you feel. Take a moment now if you're feeling stressed. Do you feel a physical sensation – or are you snappy with those around you? Are you feeling lonely and withdrawn, or are you acting out? Getting things out in the open and talking things through with a friend or family member can help you to organise your thoughts.

2 Breathe

Basic breathing exercises – like counting in for three seconds and out for five seconds – may sound simple, but will help when you get that panicky feeling.

3 Relax

Have a drifting time where you have nothing specific to do, without your phone or being in front of a screen. Perhaps write in a journal or simply look out of the window and daydream.

4 Exercise

Any form of exercise, from running to football and even yoga, can act as a stress reliever. Physical activity helps bump up the production of your brain's feel-good chemicals, called endorphins. It also helps you to sleep better. Try a few fast laps of the pool and you'll often find you've forgotten the day's worries and concentrated only on your body's movements.

5 Achieve

If you can't fix your current problem, focusing on a different problem that you *can* fix can give you a sense of accomplishment.

6 Be generous

As you're going through your day, try to see the world through other people's eyes. By getting out of your own head, you'll see life – and your problems – with a new sense of perspective. Do things for other people. Put yourself aside from time to time and help others: do the dishes, read to your siblings or call a grandparent. It makes a real difference to others and it will lift your spirits too.

And if none of that helps?

If you feel your stress is long-lasting or serious, speak to an adult, whether that be a relative or teacher. Listen carefully to the advice they give, even if you don't like what they have to say at first. Test their ideas out as an experiment – and come up with your own ideas.

Your teenage years are a period of amazing growth and change. It's likely to be stressful at times but try to stop now and then, take stock, and remember – this is all part of becoming you.

BE THE POND

When lots of emotions are swimming around inside you, it can feel overwhelming. But what if there was a simple way to calm the waters?

Imagine you were looking into a pond with all sorts of fish in it. Then imagine that each one of those fish represented a different emotion you might feel during your day. There's an angry fish, a happy fish, a sad fish, an excited fish, a bored fish, a jealous fish – all the emotions. If you were sitting in the middle of that pond with those emotional fish surrounding you, you might start to feel overwhelmed.

But what if, instead of being in the middle of this emotional storm, you could just be the whole pond? It's an idea put forward by The 100hours, an organisation encouraging young people to see how they can make a difference in the world. What if you could watch each emotion swim right by you without getting too caught up in all the swirling and splashing about? What if you could realise that although the fish are pretty emotional, the pond itself remains cool and contained?

Sometimes your emotions can feel like a big storm is building and gathering strength inside of you. But if you stop and properly acknowledge what you're feeling, taking time to recognise the emotion and name it, you might discover that the emotion eventually fades away and a different one comes along later. You may realise that you can weather the storm by simply watching it pass.

When you do this, you are learning not to identify yourself with the emotion. You don't become anxious, you simply notice that anxious feelings are present. That's because watching your emotions makes it easier to see where they're coming from and to let go of any challenging ones. And being able to notice an emotion just as it begins means you can then go on to develop a more balanced relationship with it. So next time you're feeling worried or sad about something, remember to imagine the pond, and see if the exercises over the page can help.

WATCHING YOUR EMOTIONS

At the start of term, mixed emotions can be swimming around inside you – anxiety, excitement, fear, sadness or something else. Similar to the fish in the pond, maybe you could imagine that all these emotions are running around in the playground. If you start to worry, you might feel you're the nervous fish in the pond or that you've become a bundle of worries running around the playground.

Can you remember to be the whole pond – or the playground – instead? Can you notice your worries without trying to solve all of them right away? Can you watch how your emotions seem to come and go pretty quickly, just like the students rushing around in the playground in front of you? Can you trust that you can handle these emotions, just like the playground can handle all those pupils?

If you're noticing some difficult emotions, give this exercise a go:

Close your eyes and imagine you are your schoolyard, with all your different emotions running around in it, mixing and mingling.

For each different emotion that you notice, ask yourself:

* Where in my body do I feel this emotion?

* If this emotion were an animal, what would it be?

* If this emotion were a colour, what would it be?

* What is a helpful thing I can do for myself when I start to experience this emotion?

What's it like to watch all of these emotions go by? Can you let some of them go?

NO EMOTION
LASTS FOREVER

From happiness to sadness and excitement to fear,
emotions are shifting all the time

Almost everyone experiences difficult emotions during the day. It's part of the human experience. What makes things a little more complicated is that often people have all sorts of thoughts and feelings about their feelings.

For example, when you're feeling miserable, you might tell yourself, 'I'll always be miserable.' The emotional pain might be so intense you can't imagine it fading.

When you practise mindfulness and pay closer attention to your thoughts, feelings and experiences, you'll come to see that no emotion lasts forever. In fact, if you step back and observe your emotion, you might be surprised at how quickly it starts to change.

In her book, *A Still Quiet Place For Teens,* author Amy Saltzman recommends

trying to graph or track your emotional experiences. So, grab some paper and think of feelings you might like to track. They could include anything from happiness to sadness, fear to relief, jealousy to love.

As best you can remember, over the course of a week, jot down a note of the time when an emotion begins and when it ends and, on a scale of 1 to 10, make a note of its intensity, marking how this changes over time. Disappointment, for instance, might be felt at level 8 for an hour but then slowly drop to level 3 or 4 over the course of a day or week. Anger, meanwhile, might begin at 10 but be down to zero after five minutes.

You may notice different patterns in your emotions: for you, anger may spike quickly, and then fade slowly, while sadness is more of a gentle wave. By tracking your emotions you can actually experience the impermanent nature of your emotions.

Once you have a sense of your emotional patterns, you can become more familiar with what each feeling is like as it begins, as it peaks and as it subsides. You might notice that you can 'catch' a difficult emotion in its early stages and then do something to soothe yourself, instead of letting the feeling carry you away. In this way, you can create the space needed to process your emotions and respond to situations appropriately. This will help you now and as you go through life.

THE MAGIC OF HALT

Keeping on top of your emotions can be hard, but here's one way
that might help to make sure you're in control when it matters most

Life is a complicated business and there are moments when it can be really difficult
to keep your emotions in check. Sometimes they may take over completely and you
say or do something that you didn't mean. It happens. You're not the first person to
lose control and you won't be the last. But it's good to know that there are things
you can do to make sure you're ready to deal with an important conversation or an
exam, make a big life decision or tackle something that really matters to you.

There is a checklist, called HALT, that can help you decide whether you're in the
best state of mind to approach a particular situation and, if that situation can't be
avoided, whether you need to do something to improve your chances of dealing
with it in an appropriate way.

WHAT IS HALT?

HALT stands for Hungry, Angry, Lonely, Tired. These are all feelings
that can hijack your emotions and affect the parts of the brain that
control logical thinking, reasoning and problem-solving.

If you're feeling any of these things, it can be hard to think clearly
and it's easier for your more instinctive emotions to take over. In
order to recognise and tackle your HALT areas before they start
running the show, you can ask yourself a key question when you're
facing something you need to do that's important: am I hungry,
angry, lonely or tired?

If you are, then taking action first can have a significant impact on
how you manage the situation. The sections over the page explain
what's going on in these areas and how to conquer any difficulties
they might present.

Hungry

Don't underestimate the power of hunger to mess with emotions. Without regular, balanced meals, the brain may start to become preoccupied by food and your blood sugar levels might dip, which can lead to mood swings and irritability.

Naomi Buff, a holistic nutritional wellness coach from Naomi's Kitchen, says: 'It is important to have three balanced meals a day, particularly eating a good-quality breakfast within two hours of waking up.'

She says that your choice of snacks during the day is also important as they can affect blood sugars and mood. Her suggestions include hummus with veggie sticks, homemade energy balls or rice cakes with almond butter.

Angry

If you feel angry, it can be helpful to reflect on what triggered it in the first place. Can you do something about this situation now? If yes, make a plan and take steps to put it into action – maybe you could apologise to the friend you might have upset or finish the homework that you started.

If you have to wait to put the plan into action, decide when you'll do it. If you can't do anything now, it's time to let it go and move on to something else.

Imagine blowing the problem away on a bubble or write it down on a piece of paper, rip it up and put it in the bin. Find something enjoyable and active to occupy your time and your thoughts, so you're not just going over it in your mind.

onely

Feeling lonely can seriously colour your thoughts. Being around other people generates mood-enhancing chemicals and also helps to prevent your view of life from becoming narrow and negative. If you notice your mood taking a turn for the worse and you think it may be because you're feeling lonely, make contact with someone you enjoy being around.

ired

Whether you've been overdoing it or your sleep's been disrupted by next-door's dog barking all night, tiredness can affect mood. Think about your bedtime habits. Are you going to bed early enough or waking up worried about something?

Try keeping a notebook by the side of your bed and jot down anything important you need to do or things that are worrying you. This will get those thoughts out of your head and help you get some restful sleep, knowing that none of the important details will be forgotten.

HALT YOUR PATTERNS

These aren't the only things that can affect your mood, but the HALT checklist is a great place to start. Keeping a diary of your moods (and what you do to manage them) can help you become more familiar with your emotional patterns and could even prevent some problems from arising time and time again. You might make some surprising discoveries, too – for instance, could it be that every time you get annoyed with your sibling it also happens to be when you really need to have something to eat?

UNDER PRESSURE

How to cope when family members' expectations get too much

Experiencing a bit of pressure in life is often what motivates people to strive to achieve their goals – they find themselves up against it, but push themselves harder and reap the rewards later. To succeed at anything, it helps to make an effort, apply yourself, try to stick to deadlines and take all the help and advice that's available. Even then, there's no guarantee you'll get exactly what you want at the end of it all, but at least you'll know that you gave it your best shot – that you tried.

When learning new skills, you don't just need to learn the cold, hard facts, figures or techniques, you also need the encouragement of others who've been through it before. Your parents were likely in a similar situation at one time, so you might find that they can guide you through difficult patches, highlight the pitfalls and make you realise you're not alone. But although they mean well, sometimes their attempts to spur you on can backfire and it can feel like they're piling on too much pressure. This can become overwhelming and end up doing more harm than good.

1 Great expectations
When does reasonable pressure turn into unreasonable expectation? You might think your parents or guardians are too pushy, especially when they start bragging to other people about how brilliant you are and how one day you're going to rule the world. But they might have no idea that they've stepped over the line and made you feel stressed or anxious. They might firmly believe you're capable of far more than you realise and that they're just being supportive, but what if you're doing your best and their interfering is only making things worse? If you feel they're expecting too much of you, then it's important to tell them.

2 Choose your moment
Try not to let the pressure build to the point where you suddenly snap and end up having a huge row. Remember that other people have no idea what's going on in your head unless you tell them. Your parents or family might think you're fine and just getting on with things when the reality is that you're panicking and struggling with the pressure. Wait until you're calm and not feeling so anxious and then ask if you can talk about your workload.

3 Stressful times

At times of high pressure, like exams, it often feels like your family are continually getting on at you and stating the obvious. 'Work hard and you'll succeed' – sound familiar? In the same way that teachers want the best results for their pupils, your family wants you to be well equipped to follow whatever career path you choose. So when they remind you to spend time focusing on your study and not playing around online, they aren't necessarily criticising, they're trying to motivate you.

4 Be honest

Not everyone can – or wants to be – a brain surgeon, retail chief or the next JK Rowling. Your parents or guardians might be set on you going to university, but if you've tried your hardest and feel those A* grades are out of your reach (or if you'd just prefer to do a vocational course or an apprenticeship), be honest and tell them. Everyone's different and academic performance is only one part of a person. Some students will be great at exams, others less so. Similarly, some will be natural communicators, while others struggle to read out loud in class. If the university route isn't for you, talk to your family about it and discuss other possibilities.

5 It's your future

Have a discussion and not an argument. Make sure you can get across your points clearly, which means doing research beforehand. Could it be that your parents' fears for you are unfounded and they're the ones who aren't coping with the pressure? They're looking at your future based on their own experiences, so reassure them that you have your own plans. Keeping them involved might make them worry a little less.

Take a seat and enjoy some time out
If the stress keeps building, give yourself time to clear your mind. Get yourself to a quiet space, sit comfortably – some like to be cross-legged – eyes open or closed and take long, deep breaths until you feel a little calmer. Or try our Belly Breath meditation on page 32.

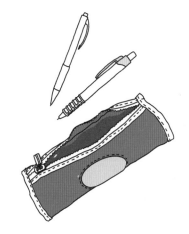

A JOURNAL FOR LIFE

Need to escape annoying siblings, sound off about your folks, muse endlessly about your one true love or work out the route to your dream job? A journal could be the answer...

It doesn't judge, doesn't laugh, doesn't tell. It just listens. That's why keeping a journal is so good. Think of your journal as a friend who never gets bored of what you have to say, who helps you to make sense of all the random thoughts that race through your head, who shares your worries, and lets you explore dreams and ambitions. That's a special person. Even better, this one will be with you for life, always able to recall and understand important moments in your life, no matter how small.

It's a precious gift from the You of the present to the You of the future.

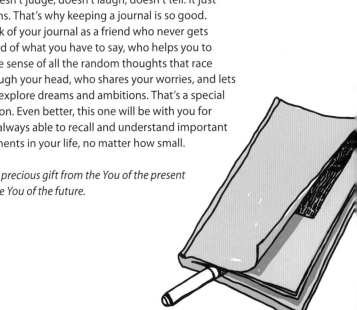

WHY START A JOURNAL?

1 It's a great way to find your voice and build inner confidence, especially at times of great change, physically and emotionally.

2 If you are working towards a goal – a special badge in Guides, say, or studying for exams – it can be useful to track your progress.

3 It can help to process and understand events (the good and also the not-so-good) and any potentially difficult emotions, worries or concerns that might surround them. (And sometimes it's good just to be able to vent your frustrations without any consequences.)

There are many issues you could explore:

* If you're feeling low, or a little lost, and don't know why, you can keep asking yourself/your journal the reasons for your feelings until you see potential answers.

* If you're worried about not being popular or interesting enough, a journal can help you to see that everyone is unique and remarkable, and that actually you have plenty to offer the world.

* If you're feeling under pressure to behave in a way that doesn't feel comfortable, a journal can be a means of finding the strength to say 'No'.

* If someone at school has stopped talking to you, a journal gives you the ideal space and opportunity to explore any potential reasons (as unreasonable as they may be), and how you feel about them. This can help you act in a more composed manner in real life.

4 It's a safe place where you can admit things that might otherwise make you feel vulnerable or ashamed (even though they shouldn't). If you're being bullied, for example, admitting it is happening to you can be incredibly hard. But once you take the first step in sharing the problem with your journal, you are better equipped to go on from there and tell a person who can help you to resolve the situation.

5 By observing patterns in your behaviour, as well as those in the people around you, it's easier to recognise that feelings change from day to day and even moment to moment. This can help you to see more clearly that just because someone's angry today, it doesn't mean they'll still be angry tomorrow.

6 It can clarify thoughts and opinions, and improve communication. By writing about subjects other than yourself, concerns you might have about the environment, for example, you are better able to tackle these large subjects in open discussions without feeling it's too big a topic.

7 Learning to feel free to write what you like, without worrying that what you've written isn't good enough, and focusing primarily on just getting things out of your head and on to the page can help with creative writing.

8 As you make note of what happens in your life, seeing it all written down can help you to appreciate the little things that make life wonderful. Your favourite song coming on the radio seconds after talking about it, for instance, or the smell of freshly mowed summer grass.

PERSONALISE YOUR JOURNAL

Any regular notebook can be used as a journal. You don't have to buy a special one. Just make it your own by writing your name on it, marking it 'Top Secret' if you like and then decorating it in your own way – use colour, stickers and pictures to make it your own. You can also buy journals that have a little padlock and key.

Internet journals are available, which are free online sites for writing your journal. But a written journal is a nice break from technology and gives your mind and imagination free space to roam.

HOW TO START A JOURNAL

A journal doesn't need to begin on a special day. It can start on a very ordinary Tuesday… in fact, that's the best time.

You could get going by describing what's around you: what you are eating or drinking; what your pet's doing; what you're going to do or what you have done with your day. Through exploring the everyday, you will find you're freer to start thinking about bigger things and looking further ahead, such as what you'd like to be doing and where you'd like to be a year from now.

TOP TIPS

* Be honest with yourself. That's how you get to know who you really are. Remember, you're not trying to impress anyone.

* Use it as a space to empty your head of thoughts. Don't put pressure on yourself to try to make it interesting – just write or draw whatever is happening, or whatever comes into your head.

* This is for your eyes only. It's your own little world and you can do and say whatever you want in it.

* If you don't have much time, just writing a few lines, or drawing a few pictures, can help you untangle thoughts and understand what's happened during the day. Don't beat yourself up if you don't write in your journal every day.

* Try to remember to date your journal entries (you can even log the time if you feel like being really detailed) as it will be helpful whenever you read them back in the future.

* If you're really not finding anything interesting at the moment then record the nature around you – even if you live in a city, what have you seen? A fox? Pigeons? Snails? A rose? Then try to describe how seeing these things made you feel.

* Have fun! It's a place for your imagination to run wild. Explore all your ideas, fantasies and feelings. And don't limit yourself to words – use drawings, sketches, stickers, pictures, doodles. Anything you like to make it yours.

HOW TO HANDLE ANGER

How does anger feel to you? Like a hot fire raging in your belly, or an inner scream demanding to be heard? Everyone gets angry sometimes. It's how you deal with it that's important

Hit the ceiling, blow up, have a meltdown – there are many ways to describe the point when anger erupts. Feeling cross is a regular emotion as well as a healthy one, because it can highlight problems that need addressing. But there are also times when it can hurt other people. It isn't easy to take back spiteful words shouted in the heat of the moment, no matter how genuinely they're regretted.

So what's to be done when that sudden urge to act out anger arises? Firstly, remember that your personal feelings are important. You may feel a real sense of injustice about being grounded by a parent, being given a detention by a teacher or ignored by a friend. Anger can also be used as a mask, a way of hiding vulnerable feelings of hurt, fear or grief. Try to work out the real reason you felt angry – maybe you thought you weren't being listened to, were worried about not being good enough, or weren't receiving enough support.

Simple factors such as what you eat and the amount of sleep you get can make a difference to how easily you can control your emotions. Eating sugar-loaded drinks and sweets can produce an artificial 'high' that is followed by a low, when you're more likely to feel irritable. Not sleeping enough can also make emotions go awry, so try to establish a relaxing evening routine that makes it easier to nod off.

When anger is directed at a particular person, it can be a good plan to wait a while before talking to them. You may desperately want them to understand how you feel, but anger can cloud what you want to say and transform justly held opinions into words and sentences you don't mean.

Anger makes it difficult to think clearly and communicate effectively. When you're wound up, try these tips to help put you in a better frame of mind to explore and tackle what made you so angry in the first place:

1 Recognise your anger signs and then count to 10

A fast heart rate and quick breaths can indicate that anger is rising. Other signs include tension in the shoulders or clenching of the fists. When you find yourself getting angry, take long, slow breaths, and count to 10. This gives you a chance to think more clearly before reacting out of anger.

2 Talk things over with someone you trust

Do you have a friend or family member who is a good listener? Talking over how you feel can help you to let go of angry feelings. If anger is getting in the way of your life, you might want to confide in a school counsellor. They can teach you ways to cope with anger.

3 Engage in physical activity

Anger can manifest itself as a tightness in the chest or throat. Exercise can help to ease this and to release angry feelings. Getting moving can be a great way to let go of pent-up emotions, so think about going for a walk or practising some yoga.

4 Discover mindfulness

Mindfulness can teach you to watch your thoughts as a calm observer rather than getting caught up in them, and acting them out. Practising regularly can help to prevent anger and make it easier to stay calm when the feeling arises.

5 Do something fun or creative

What gives you a sense of joy? Meeting a friend, having a dance, drawing a picture or watching a movie? Doing things you love can shift your mood.

Belly breath
AWARENESS
MEDITATION

Find a quiet place where you won't be disturbed for at least
10 minutes. Sit comfortably on the floor.

**Place your palms on your lower belly, resting them there
loosely without tension. Now close your eyes and breathe deeply
and slowly, in through your nose and out through your mouth.**

Feel your belly move up and down as you breathe in and out.

**Focus just on that for a while and, very soon, the chatter
in your mind should ease (it takes a lot of practice for it to get
even close to stopping altogether).**

Once the volume of your thoughts has been turned down,
focus your awareness on other sensations. Pay attention to each
part of your body in turn – feel the pressure of the floor, the touch of
your clothes against your skin, and the sound of your breath
as you gently inhale and exhale. Relax your shoulders, then
your arms, then your hands. Feel the rise and fall of your belly.

**When the time is right, slowly and calmly open your eyes.
You're ready to go on with your day.**

THINK TWICE

When something bad happens to you, ancient survival instincts can come into play – but mostly it's better to think before you act

Have you heard of the fight-or-flight reflex? It's the way humans are wired to react to a perceived threat or harmful encounter. Some people counter-attack and others look for a way to escape. It's something that's helped people to survive on this planet for as long as they have. After all, your ancient ancestors would have had to deal with some pretty scary situations – sabre-toothed tiger, anyone?

Thankfully life has moved on a lot since prehistoric times. Today the world is more complex and, even though old instincts remain, sometimes the scarier situations you find yourself in require different ways of dealing with them.

HOW WOULD YOU REACT?

Survival instinct

There are still some circumstances where those old survival instincts will kick in. Imagine someone puts you in danger. In this case, it's natural to choose, without even really thinking about it, between fighting against or flying from the situation.

If someone pushed you into a wall, for instance, perhaps you'd push back or run away. If you were out riding your bike and a friend started riding dangerously, swerving into you and nearly knocking you off, maybe you'd shout at them to stop.

These responses are driven purely by survival instincts. They help, in a split second, to assess a potentially dangerous situation and ensure self-protection.

But while the fight-or-fight reflex, which stems from a need for self-preservation, makes sense if you're in physical danger, it seems less appropriate in a scenario that involves feelings.

Think before you act

Imagine a different type of situation. Your best friend makes a comment that upsets you, or borrows one of your favourite dresses and accidentally spills something on it. Would you react in the same way, by shouting, pushing or running away from the scene?

Although some of the feelings might be the same – anger, fear and hurt can all cause a knotted feeling in the stomach that leads to lashing out – a calmer reaction might have a better outcome. Maybe it's better to pause, take a deep breath, process those feelings and explain to your friend that you're upset, and why.

Let's compare what the reaction and the response to this situation might be:

Friend *'Here's your dress back, but I splashed something on it, and the stain won't come out. I'm sorry, I didn't mean to.'*

You 1 *'What? How? That was my favourite dress and now it's ruined. I hate you.'*

OR

You 2 *'I'm really upset about that dress. It was my favourite and now it's ruined. I know you didn't mean to do it, but I'd prefer that you didn't borrow my clothes in future.'*

The first 'you' is reacting from the gut, but it could make a situation that is already unfortunate even worse and lead to more distress. The second 'you' is still making their feelings known, but in a way that's less likely to add fuel to the fire.

Another example: you get a bad grade on a maths test at school:

You 1 *'I hate maths. It's the dumbest subject ever, and I hate my teacher. She's always picking on me, and I bet she failed me on purpose.'*

OR

You 2 *'That's so disappointing, I'm really unhappy. Maybe I'll ask my teacher about it and see what I can do to get a better result next time.'*

The frustration about the bad grade completely takes over the first 'you'. Although venting in this way might make you feel better in that moment, it's not going to have any benefit in the long term. Responding to the disappointment is what the second 'you' does. This involves acknowledging how you feel and pinpointing what needs to be done to avoid it happening again.

Emotional maturity

The ability to respond to situations gets easier with experience. If a toddler is told that they can't have ice cream until they finish their dinner, they'll possibly have a tantrum and throw a spoon at the wall. They don't realise it's making their desired outcome even less likely.

A child of six or seven, however, is smarter. They might sulk a bit, but know that after eating carrots (not their favourite), there'll be something altogether tastier on the dinner table.

In other words, teaching yourself to respond, rather than react to disappointment – or hurt feelings – is much more likely to make the end result a positive one.

Don't give yourself a hard time if you do react, rather than respond, to a situation. Everybody has the occasional outburst – just try to follow up with a more considered response after you've given yourself time to process what's happened, how you feel about it and what steps you can take to avoid it being repeated. Although you shouldn't expect, however, that it'll always result in ice cream.

`IT'S NOT WHAT HAPPENS TO YOU, BUT HOW YOU REACT TO IT THAT MATTERS`

Epictetus

FACEBOOK FAREWELLS

Unfriending someone on Facebook can seem a big step to take, but there are ways to make it as stress-free as possible

You've been patient for weeks and weeks, trying as much as possible not to get drawn into their Facebook rants. But you just can't take them any more. It's time to delete that annoying online friend. So how do you unfriend someone? And how do you do it without causing an argument?

You see, while it's easy to notch up hundreds of friends online, it could be that when you scan your buddy list, you realise you don't know some of your connections at all or simply no longer want to have their images and statements popping up on your feed. Alternatively, you might want to restrict your Facebook crew to only your closest friends and family members, or remove someone with whom you've recently fallen out.

Whatever the reason, if you're thinking of removing someone, there are a few things to bear in mind to keep it as worry-free as possible…

Be clear about your reasons
Make sure you know why you want to remove them and that you're not going to change your mind soon after. It's easy to fall out with someone and remove them in a moment of anger, but you'll look silly when you decide to send a friend request again after you've made up.

If you're unsure whether to remove them, write down the reasons why you're considering it. For example, 'We're not friends anymore,' or 'I want to remove people I've not spoken to for over a year,' or 'I'm finding their posts inappropriate.' So that you're 100 per cent sure, take a day or two to consider your decision.

Remember that most people won't notice or even care
You may not want to unfriend someone because you're worried about how you'll look or how the other person will react when they realise they've been removed. The truth is though, most of the time they won't even notice. It's easy to think people register what you do online, but more often than not they're too concerned with their own lives to see what others are doing.

DELETING SOMEONE ON FACEBOOK IS SIMPLE

* Go to the person's timeline or profile.

* Click the 'Friends' button.

* Click 'Unfriend' in the menu.

* Find the 'Remove from Friends' button and click it.

* Take a deep breath. That wasn't so hard, was it?

To unfriend or unfollow?

If you don't want to fully remove a friend or are feeling anxious about the whole thing, you can choose to unfollow that person instead. This means you'll technically still be friends and able to visit each other's profiles, but their posts won't automatically appear in your feed.

To do this, head to their profile, and untick the 'Following' box under their profile picture. Alternatively, when they post, click the three dots to the right of their message and a menu will come up allowing you to then unfollow them.

If you don't want them seeing any of your posts, go to your privacy settings and click on 'Who can see your future posts?'. Here you add people from your friend list and prevent them seeing your updates.

Be brave

Decluttering Facebook friends can be beneficial for mental wellbeing. If those you deleted live far away, you probably won't have to deal with them again. It may be best to prepare for people who do notice to ask you why you removed them. You'll have to decide whether to tell them the truth or brush it off as a spot of decluttering to leave only people you see regularly. It may be awkward, but you made the decision to remove them and probably rarely see them, so stick with your decision. It may feel uncomfortable, but they – and you – will survive.

It's okay to look after yourself

It's natural to feel guilty if you're unfriending someone but remember why you've decided to remove them. Instead, focus on friendships you want to nurture and go back to Facebook being a positive experience for you, sharing it with people you know and like. Consider how easily you used to add people as friends and how you might be more careful in future. It's good to value your privacy and to know the people on your Facebook list.

HOW TO COPE IF YOU'VE BEEN REMOVED

If someone you like deletes you from their friends list, it may hurt at first. To start with, consider if they're a close friend you see often or just an online acquaintance.

If it's a 'real-life' friend and someone you thought you were close to, you might want to ask them why they've hit the Unfriend button and see whether you can repair the relationship (if that's what you want).

If it's an online-only friend, consider the kinds of posts you've been making and whether you think your online behaviour could have prompted their decision. If you're sure your posts have been A-OK, accept they might simply be decluttering their friends list based on what they want at the moment and that it's not personal.

It might sting, but you have other friends who are more deserving of your attention. Try to focus on them. Remember, it's better to have a small group of close friends than hundreds of people you don't really know anyway.

'IF YOU HAVE ONE TRUE FRIEND, YOU HAVE MORE THAN YOUR SHARE'

#UNFOLLOW

Thomas Fuller

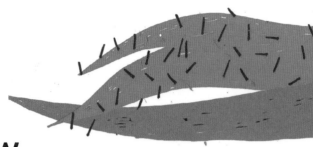

FOLLOW
THE LEADER

Don't be daunted if you're put in charge –
embrace the opportunity and shine

Are you the kind of person who thrives
on stepping up and leading groups and
teams? Or are you the type who prefers
to remain in the background as much
as possible, following someone else?

Some people are born leaders and
have no worries about being at the
head of a team or a group, whether
as a sports captain or head girl or
boy. For others, just the thought of
being in charge and having that extra
responsibility can trigger anxious
feelings – what if you make the wrong
decision? What if people think you're
doing a bad job?

*What skills do you need to be a leader
and can everybody develop them?
Here are some tips about taking charge,
gaining the trust of your team and being
the best leader you can be...*

1 Find your confidence

To have been chosen as a leader or captain is a huge honour – and you wouldn't have been selected if people didn't think you were up to it. Yes, it may be nerve-racking, but remember everyone feels like that at first. Embrace those nerves and take on the challenge.

Be careful not to let that confidence slip into arrogance, however, otherwise the people you lead won't respect you for long. Instead, be calm, respectful and proud of the position you've been given and give it your best shot.

2 Look to your role models for inspiration

Consider leaders you know of and keep them in mind as role models. What do you respect about them? Is it because they're fair and supportive? Are they good at public speaking or motivating others? Model yourself on their behaviours, but make the role your own using your skills. Be the best version of you, not anyone else.

3 Put in the effort

The most important role as a captain or leader is to lead by example. Your teammates or group will look up to you and there will be times when they'll need your guidance and advice. They'll also want to see you as the person giving 100 per cent to whatever you do and being passionate, enthusiastic and proud.

If you don't work hard, neither will your team. Be positive, motivational and demonstrate a supportive, fair attitude. The chances are people will want to copy you in future.

4 Harness the team's strengths

Your role is to lead your team to success and help them reach the top. Often this is only possible if all members of the group pull together as one.

Don't be afraid to delegate tasks. Take a tip from the most successful leaders: use the individual strengths of others around you to create the best team.

5 Communicate clearly

Part of being a good leader is knowing how to motivate people, especially when the going gets tough and they really need it. For example, if a team member has made a mistake, you need to be able to let them know they can improve and encourage them to look forward rather than get hung up on it.

If your team's losing, you'll have to be the one to inspire them to remain hungry for the win, determined and resilient. Consider some inspirational words and positive phrases that you think might work for your group.

6 Deal with conflict

There'll often be disagreements within a team or group. As the leader, you'll have to deal with them. This might be the toughest part of being a captain because it may mean telling someone they've made a mistake or resolving a tricky issue. Consider your body language, tone and words when you speak to them and be sure to refer to the questionable behaviour rather than criticise the person.

7 Accept criticism

Your team may not like everything you do or every single decision you make, but be confident, positive and believe in yourself. If you can, others will too, whether they agree with your approach or not. Nobody is perfect and any role takes time and practice – try not to let setbacks prevent you from being the great leader you were destined to be. It's a fantastic opportunity and will help boost your confidence for whatever you choose to do after school or college.

HOW TO BE A LEADER

* Speak up and don't be afraid to put yourself forward, even if it's in a room full of strangers. Make the most of the opportunity.

* Consider your body language when speaking to others. Think about how you stand and move, plus your eye contact. Make an effort to seem approachable and be interested in what others have to say.

* Always listen and accept points. When you're in a group, it's important not to dominate. Let others lead as well.

* Respect others' opinions. People are different and that's okay. Try to see things from their perspective.

* Be enthusiastic and interesting when talking to groups. Try to consider who you're speaking to and how you can engage them, even during the boring bits.

LET'S HAVE A DEBATE...

...but keep it calm, reasoned and helpful. In other words, here's how to clearly and calmly express your point of view – even when others strongly disagree

Arguing, debating, differences of opinion – they're a regular part of everyday life as people express their views and wishes to others. It could be about the best way to approach an essay, whether student grants should be scrapped or who's the best person to lead the country. Whatever the subject, it's not the same as rowing with someone just because they get on your nerves (like a sibling, for example!) – it's about getting across what's important to you in a thoughtful, sensible way.

If you want to convince someone of your argument, it pays to be prepared. Decide what your point is and how you're going to defend it if others take the opposite view. If you watch politicians on TV, they're practised in the art of arguing because interviewers are constantly examining their policies and making them explain their viewpoints. To win their argument, they might repeat rehearsed points – sometimes sidestepping the question they've been asked. Other times, they'll tackle the subject head-on and give evidence to back up their viewpoint.

In your life, you might feel strongly about a subject or something that personally affects you, whether you're a passionate vegan or a fan of a particular style of music. It's okay to share these interests, but try to remember everyone sees things based on their own life experiences. They might not agree with you – nor you with them – but hopefully you can learn from and respect each other.

THE ART OF ARGUING

The art of debate can be viewed as old-fashioned, but it involves mastering life skills that can be useful throughout life, and unlearnable in other ways:

* The confidence to speak out about what you believe in, and make sense.
* The construction of a logical argument.
* The ability to notice inconsistencies in someone else's argument.
* The capacity to read other people's reactions.
* A willingness to hear other people's arguments.
* A readiness to question and analyse your own opinions.
* An ability to think on your feet.

IT'S TIME TO TALK

Here are some tips to bear in mind when you want to put forward an argument in a calm and collected way…

DO

Articulate
Be clear about the point you're trying to make, which means rehearsing your thoughts well in advance. Imagine what people are likely to say to shoot down your argument and prepare how you will answer your critics.

Be concise
Choose your words carefully to get across the full impact of what you're saying. The sooner you get to the point, the better – keep it short and sharp.

Respond
It's important to acknowledge the other person's point of view, even if you totally disagree with it. Use phrases like, 'I get what you're saying but…' or 'I understand but that's not really what we're discussing…' and bring it back to your point.

Study the other person
By properly listening to the other person, you can get to fully understand their beliefs, as well as the strengths and weaknesses of their argument.

Be confident
A large part of bringing people around to your viewpoint is about appearing confident and knowledgeable. If you seem convinced by what you're saying, others are more likely to agree with you.

DON'T

Get too bogged down in detail
Many people make the mistake of going into too much detail before getting to their point, by which time others will have got bored. Stick firmly to the subject and avoid any detail that may weaken your argument.

Get thrown off course
Other people will try to interrupt you with their own views, often raising their voices to speak over you. Don't shout back or get flustered, just take a breath and repeat what you were saying in a slow and steady voice.

Run out of steam
While you're speaking, try to think ahead and visualise your next point before you finish the current one so that you speak in a continuous flow. This will make your knowledge on the subject sound far wider.

Get angry
Losing your temper and turning nasty is a surefire way to lose an argument, as you'll end up appearing impatient and aggressive. You don't want to look like a toddler throwing a tantrum and flinging their toys out of the pram.

Sulk
If you feel you're losing the argument, don't start sulking – it will come across as an immature way of reacting to criticism. Believe in your opinion, but also listen to what the other person is saying. If you feel they've made a good point, tell them that – it doesn't mean you've lost.

HUNG UP ABOUT PHONE CALLS?

WhatsApp and Snapchat are great tools for communicating with friends, but learning how to have a confident phone conversation is an important skill to master, too

WHAT'S THE PROBLEM?

If you're nervous about using the phone, you might worry about making a call, put it off, or avoid the task completely by messaging or emailing instead. When on the phone, you might find your voice suddenly dries up, you don't know what to say or you just can't seem to get your words out in the right order. These are all common signs of being nervous or anxious. Although these feelings are usually temporary and disappear once you've made the call, worry about talking on the phone can mean you forget to ask about the thing you called for, you don't fully take in what's being said or you miss out entirely by not making the call in the first place.

Why do people worry about phone calls?
Phone calls are no longer the everyday habit they once were. The rapid development of digital technologies over the past two decades means it's now more common to 'talk' via text or instant messaging. You might not make frequent phone calls and, as with anything, the less familiar you are with a particular task, the more likely you are to lack confidence when you do have to do it.

Speaking on the telephone can seem more challenging than other forms of communication. Social media, email and texts give you time to consider what you want to say. There's less pressure to respond immediately. You have space to think about what people might really mean and what your answer is going to be. On the phone, however, even brief pauses can feel awkward and uncomfortable. You might feel rushed into giving a response.

Body language is more important than you'd think
Phone calls are, of course, different from face-to-face interaction. In conversation, people use lots of non-verbal clues – such as eye contact, facial expression, body language, gesture and context – to help them convey their message and understand the other person.

When speaking on the phone, these helpful signals – that might be taken for granted when you're chatting to someone in person – are missing, leaving those on the call with some guesswork to do. Researchers suggest we might understand only seven per cent of a message from the actual words heard. The remaining 93 per cent of deciphering comes from how these words are conveyed (for example, tone of voice) and contextual clues (for example, body language). It's no wonder communicating on the phone seems tricky.

Why is the phone necessary?

Although the phone might not be your preferred or most popular choice of communication, it's still useful to learn how to make a phone call with confidence. Having conversations in this way can strengthen relationships. Hearing a friend's voice can help you to feel more connected than simply seeing their words appear on a screen.

Sometimes the phone is the quickest way to get the information you need – when you start working, it could also be essential. As with anything, often all it takes is a little bit of practice to get you feeling a whole lot more confident.

HOW TO MAKE MORE CONFIDENT PHONE CALLS

1 **Stand tall**. Although the other person on the call can't see you, your body language still makes a big difference to your attitude – and they can pick up on that. Standing up to make a phone call might help you feel more confident. Distribute your weight evenly across both feet, roll your shoulders back and down and take a few slow breaths. Smile when you're speaking to release tension and feel more relaxed.

2 **Prepare**. Before the call, make notes of any questions you want to ask so you have a reminder if your mind suddenly goes blank. Have a pen and paper to hand to jot down important information during the call.

3 **Rehearse important conversations**. If you have an important or significant call to make, such as enquiring about a part-time job, try to practise first with a supportive friend or family member. You might feel a little silly, but role play helps to improve confidence and performance. Ask for feedback on what you did well and what you should consider doing differently.

4 **Remove distractions**. It can be difficult to concentrate when there's background noise. Move to a quieter place to make your call.

5 **Don't take it personally**. It can be easy to misinterpret other people's intentions without the usual conversational clues. If you receive a short or less than helpful response, remember the other person might be tired, preoccupied or, like you, also dislike using the phone. Always remain polite, ask for the information you need and finish the call in a pleasant way.

6 **'Catch' your worries**. The listener can't see your red face or shaking hands. They're also unlikely to notice simple slips of the tongue or a croaky voice. It's easy to worry about things that others don't even register.

7 **Ask for repetition or clarification when you need it**. Don't be afraid to say you didn't hear or understand something. It happens all the time on the phone. Try saying: 'I didn't quite catch that. Could you repeat it, please?' or 'Would you be able to explain that again, please?'

SNAP HAPPY

Taking pictures can be a wonderful calming experience. All you need to get started is a basic camera, an open mind and a little patience

When you take a photograph, not only does it allow you to capture and hold onto memories, it can change the way you see things and make the everyday seem amazing. That's because it gives you the opportunity to stop thinking and really see what's in front of you. Not sure what that means? Here's an example. Pretend you're standing before a mountain with your camera ready to go. You've been there a while, your feet are getting cold and your mind starts wandering. 'What can I take a photo of that will be really good? All the ones I've taken so far are rubbish. What if I take one and it's so good it wins a competition? Maybe I can even sell some…' When your mind drifts off like this, you have lost touch with your surroundings: the mountain, the clouds, the way the light is hitting the peak. Your concentration has gone, and you're no longer focusing on the subject you're trying to photograph.

camera

Here are three ways to help bring your mind back to your subject...

1 Turn on your super-focus
Take an everyday object and look at it more closely. Choose something that wouldn't normally be thought of as photo-worthy: a toothbrush, coffee cup or cheese grater, for example. For the next few minutes keep your camera close by, but switched off. Give your full attention to the subject, noticing texture, patterns, shapes and shadows and how they relate to each other. View it from every angle; trace its contours with your fingers, use a mirror to see fresh viewpoints. Now, without trying to create a 'good' photograph, pick up your camera and start shooting. Repeat the exercise with a stretch of pavement, or even a patch of flooring. The results can be fantastic.

2 Feel the light
Often the environment you're in can affect how you feel, and when you're trying to take a photograph, light is particularly important. Look around you and ask yourself where the light is coming from. Is it hard or soft, warm or cold, bright or dim? Is the contrast high or low? How does it make you feel? Maybe the light is so warm that it reminds you of a fun family holiday – does this feeling affect the photograph you're about to take?

3 Get connected
Next time you want to photograph something, stop for a minute and think about how it connects to the rest of the world. Take a tree, for example. Find a spot in front of a huge, gnarled one and sit at its base. Rest your gaze on the trunk and think about all the forces that come together to help it live: the roots that absorb moisture from the ground, the trunk that holds up its branches while transporting nutrients, the bark that protects it from attack. Think about the sunlight the tree needs to trigger photosynthesis, the rain it needs for water and the wind that scatters its seeds. When you think about it, everything is connected. What else could you try this with?

`EVERYTHING HAS BEAUTY,
BUT NOT EVERYONE SEES IT´

Confucius

NOVEL PASTIME

Step into new worlds, see a different point of view, travel on adventures, spend time with beloved characters. How? Bookworms with teetering TBR (To Be Read) piles already know that a good book can change the way you think about things. By opening a novel you can allow yourself to laugh, cry, be distracted from problems and take time to be still

Read on to find out how it could become your life-long passion...

GETTING STARTED

1 Find your source material
If you're going to read a lot of books, you'll probably want to look beyond high-street bookstores. The school or local library and second-hand shops are all great places to find cheap, pre-read options. You could even try book-swaps with some friends.

2 Use social media
Although reading is usually a solitary activity, there's a big community of bloggers and vloggers out there who love to talk about their latest finds and offer book recommendations.

3 Make it a day out
Keep an eye on local literature festivals or bookshops for in-store author events. There are several festivals for YA (Young Adult) readers held in London every summer. They're usually packed with panels of authors talking about their books, which they'll also autograph.

HOW ABOUT A READING CHALLENGE?

It's easy to get stuck in a rut reading the same author or type of book. If you'd like to try some new authors, experiment with different types of writing or if you're just the kind of person who likes to have a target and a checklist, why not try one of these reading challenges:

Challenge One Read:

* A classic novel
* A magazine
* A book that's been made into a movie
* A graphic novel
* A funny book

Challenge Two Read:

* A newspaper
* A book you own but you've never read
* A book recommended by a friend
* A book with fewer than 200 pages
* A poem

Challenge Three Read:

* A book set in another country
* A short story
* A book that has won a prize
* A non-fiction book
* A book with magic in it

Challenge Four Read:

* A book set more than 50 years ago
* A book based on a myth or folk tale
* A book set in a school or college
* A sci-fi fantasy
* A book your parents loved when they were your age

Challenge Five Read:

* A book with a number in the title
* A book with a yellow cover
* A book with a one-word title
* A book with a colour in the title
* A book written by an author with the same first name or surname as you

Challenge Six Over to you...
Write your own reading challenge list for you and your friends or family using new ideas or picking your favourite suggestions from the five challenges.

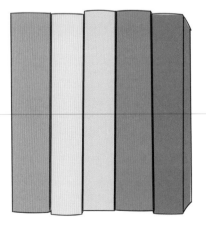

YOU CAN ADD TO THE CHALLENGES WITH WAYS TO READ

Read a chapter:

* Outside
* To a pet
* Doing all the dialogue in silly voices
* Wearing pyjamas
* Under a duvet with a torch
* To a neighbour or grandparent
* In a whisper
* Wearing a hat
* Standing on your head
* In a cosy cafe
* Singing every other page

Is it okay to give up on a book?

Yes. You don't expect to like everyone you meet in real life or love every TV programme or film you see – it's the same with books. Some will thrill you, while others will leave you cold. If you give a book a go but can't get on with it, pick another one. One day you might return to a book that didn't grab you and find that you love it – but there's no need to fret about it now.

JOIN A BOOK CLUB

This is a great way to be introduced to books that you might not have picked yourself, but that you end up really liking. It's also a way to discuss themes and ideas with other people who are as passionate as you are about books.

You can often find book clubs arranged in a college or local council library, where members are generally given between a fortnight and a month to read the book. If you can't find a book club to join, think about setting one up with your friends and then taking turns to host it (you could even theme it according to the chosen book with food, drink and outfits). Sometimes, a publisher will include discussion points in the book on its website. If not, here are a few general questions to get you started:

* Did you enjoy this book? Why? Why not?

* Did you get hooked into the story immediately?

* What do you think were the main themes?

* What did you want to happen to the central characters after the end of the book?

* Who would you pick to play the characters in a movie adaptation?

* How did the characters change throughout the story?

* What was your favourite passage?

* If you could ask the author one question, what would it be?

* What new things did you learn?

'A BOOK IS A DREAM YOU HOLD IN YOUR HANDS'

Neil Gaiman

NEED A MOMENT?

If you find yourself feeling anxious before a maths test, angry after a squabble with a sibling or confused because a friend's blanked you, take a pause, breathe slowly and try this calming exercise (if you can find a quiet place where you won't be disturbed it's even more appealing)...

* Place one hand flat in front of you – this could be on your desk, the kitchen table, the bed, the top of your tablet, or even your lap.

* Spread your fingers widely and evenly.

* Take a deep breath.

* Now, with the forefinger of your other hand, begin tracing your outstretched hand. As you draw your hand, feel any worried thoughts lift and float away. Focus on the feeling and motion of your forefinger as it calmly traces round the thumb and each of the fingers.

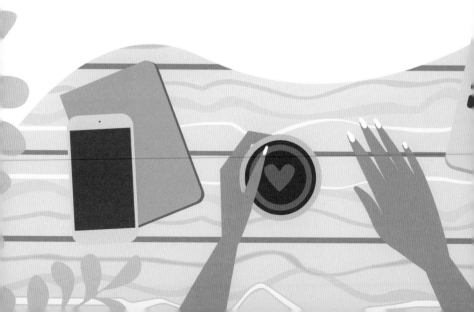

* Start at the inner point of your wrist and slowly trace around the outside edge of your thumb. When you reach the tip, pause and breathe. Then follow the line down the inside of the thumb to the point where it meets the forefinger.

* Again, pause and breathe, before slowly tracing along the facing line of the forefinger to the tip. Pause and breathe once more before continuing to trace the line down the opposite side of the finger.

* Repeat the pausing, breathing and tracing for the middle, ring and little fingers before coming to rest at the outer edge of the wrist of your outstretched hand.

* Take a deep, calming breath. You're ready to go on with your day.

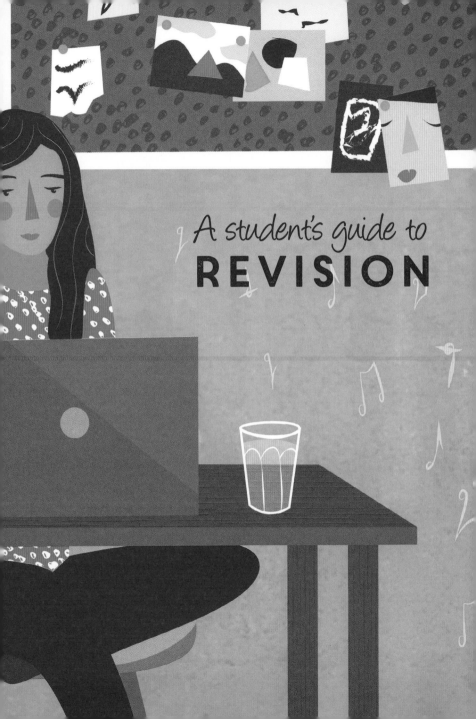

A student's guide to
REVISION

Exams. Just saying the word is enough to make some people shiver. They're anxiety inducing and teachers and parents always remind you of the importance of doing your best in them. Unfortunately, there's no escaping them (exams, that is) – but there are ways to revise properly and cope with any stress. Here's what you need to know if you want to keep a cool head while you're studying and on the actual day...

1 Get organised

The first thing to do is to create a revision timetable, because as the saying goes: 'Fail to prepare, then prepare to fail.' It may sound negative, but it's true. There's nothing worse than going into an exam knowing you've not studied.

Find out all the dates of the exams, or at least have a rough idea, so you can create a weekly plan. Consider when you have free time and what nights and weekends you can study. Then start allocating free time to the exam or different subjects, spreading out the different topics you need to cover.

2 Be realistic

Planning 12 hours of revision on a Saturday because you've nothing in your diary might look good on paper, but be realistic about the amount of time you can devote to studying. If you start revising early, you can do little and often. When planning a revision timetable, you need to ensure you have enough downtime to relax and do things you really enjoy. You'll be a better student because of it. Too much continuous work will lead to you becoming stressed and tired, so ensure you look after your brain and give it a break.

3 Know your stuff

Your teachers are there to help you, so if they haven't already, ask them exactly what you need to know. Instead of writing 'English' in your revision timetable, write 'Revise the character of Romeo' or 'Develop descriptive writing skills'. Break down the timetable into time slots for each subject so you can tick these off when they're done. Make it more visual by using different colours for different subjects, topics or free time.

4 Be kind to yourself

The lead-up to exams can be stressful at times so it's important you look after yourself physically and mentally. Exercise regularly so your blood circulates faster, your brain gets more oxygen and productivity increases. You will probably find it gives you more energy. Remember to take time out to do things you find relaxing – play sports or video games, sing, do yoga, paint or even knit.

5 Stay positive

Going into your exams with a positive frame of mind will give you a boost. The important thing is to do the best you can. If things don't go to plan, don't fret or panic and certainly don't give up. At the end of the day, exams are one stepping stone in life. There will always be many options available, however well you do. Just make sure you give it your all. Good luck!

'YOU NEVER FAIL UNTIL YOU STOP TRYING'

Albert Einstein

WAYS TO STUDY

Different people learn in different ways, so it may be a case of trial and error as you work out what's best for you. The good news is, there are many things to try...

1 Complete past papers

Have a go at past questions and ask your teacher to mark them so you can see what you're doing well and what needs improving. You can search online for past papers or create your own exam-style questions when you're familiar with how they're written.

2 Make a note

Some people find re-reading their old notes on a subject helps them to revise, while others prefer reading revision books and then condensing the information into key notes. Some students do this process several times to ensure the information stays in their brains.

3 Display your ideas

In the lead-up to an exam, put key words around your room on Post-it notes so even subconsciously the ideas are going into your head as you see them regularly.

4 Be creative

If you're feeling artistic and want a break from writing, create posters to put up on your walls, highlighting key ideas. You can also make mind maps of information or spider diagrams.

5 Sing!

Record yourself reading your notes onto your phone so you can listen to them on the way to school. It's another way of going over notes and it can feel less boring. Some students like creating revision videos or even songs or raps to help them remember topics. Think how many songs you can sing despite not hearing them for years. Go on, make up some tunes and add some academic lyrics.

6 Use family and friends

Create a quiz. Get your family to ask you questions on subjects you've been revising. Or, as your friends will also be feeling the same stress, organise a revision evening where you help each other.

MUSIC FOR YOUR EARS

You've got your books, your notes, a good set of stationery and a hot drink – you're all set to begin your revision session but, with a recent study showing that 94 per cent of students have music playing in the background while they revise, you may be wondering what to put on your playlist to maximise your study potential

Classical, surely?

For some time, there's been a popular theory that listening to classical music is a certain route to success. This is largely thanks to Dr Frances Rauscher, who conducted an experiment in 1993 where she discovered the 'Mozart Effect'. She found that participants performed better at tasks when they completed them while listening to Mozart than they did to a monotonous voice or silence.

What she actually recorded was that their improved performance lasted around 10 to 15 minutes and that the effect only applied to specific types of tasks. Unfortunately her findings were taken out of context and generalised by the media, which claimed that listening to Mozart could 'make you clever' and that listening to classical music from an early age could improve academic performance. As it turns out, the relationship between music and brain-power doesn't appear to be quite so straightforward, but that's not to say there's no relationship at all.

In fact, the effect of music on the brain – and on memory in particular – is profound and can be long-lasting. There's still a lot of debate around exactly why this is, but many experts believe it's at least partly because music evokes a strong emotional response, and psychologists have demonstrated time and again that positive emotions can increase the ability to remember and recall information.

So if not Mozart, then what?

Just as positive emotions can boost your ability to create memories, negative emotions can have the reverse effect. With this in mind, experts suggest that you should listen to something you enjoy and that puts you in a good mood. Ideally you're after a playlist that's calming and uplifting.

George Hammond-Hagan, CEO and founder of Studytracks, a company that specialises in creating audio tracks to aid study, says: 'Music is what's known as a "mood modifier" whereby it puts you in exactly the right, optimised state to be able to learn. All those lyrics you have in your head – you didn't try to learn them, you just did, because of repetition and opportunity. The rest is down to the brain and music working together.'

The sound of silence

Of course, you may be one of the six per cent of students who prefer not to listen to anything at all and there's certainly research to support the idea that silence may well be the best soundtrack for study. While music does stimulate the brain, music with lyrics can, according to some experts, interrupt and distract the process of learning. As well as that, there's a danger that a piece of music with too much of an association with something other than study could prove to be counter-productive – it's great to be reminded of your last holiday, but perhaps not when you're trying to concentrate on work.

A word of warning

Before you make up a revision playlist including all of your favourite songs, be aware that these tunes will probably one day remind you of exam preparation. Music to revise to now may one day bring you out in a cold sweat when it takes you back to battling with trigonometry or desperately trying to remember quotes from Shakespeare's *Much Ado About Nothing*. Music memory is a powerful thing after all!

But, whatever the scientists say, you know what works for you and what doesn't. The most important thing is that you listen to something that makes you feel good, and that you don't use your whole revision session up on choosing your music.

Five classical pieces to listen to while studying

* *Pastoral Suite*, Lars-Erik Larsson

* *A Beautiful Mind*, James Horner

* *Academic Festival Overture*, Johannes Brahms

* *The Hours*, Philip Glass

* *Etudes*, Claude Debussy

* Also, try browsing YouTube and Spotify for study playlists from a wide variety of genres, including nature sounds

TAKE THE PLUNGE

Swimming is a full body exercise and one of the best ways of keeping your body – and mind – happy and healthy. So go on, dive in

Everyone needs some solace. Some vital 'me' time. Getting away from the pressures of school, family, friends and social media is vital. A break from the norm – time to empty the mind, relax and almost acquire a meditative state – can work wonders.

So where can one find this magic pill-like quality? Easy. At your local swimming pool. It's true. You might laugh at the idea of physical exercise as an elixir, but as well as the enhanced health properties swimming can provide – of which there are many – there are a raft of other reasons why taking up swimming now, or improving your skills in the water, might be the best decision you make.

Feel calm and free

Psychotherapist Rebecca McCann, says studies have shown a positive effect on self-image, winning friends and self-esteem. 'When you think about swimming,' she says, 'the very fact that we are being held by the water is calming for most. It's a sensory sport – the sensation of the water soothes and the feeling of weightlessness can be energising and freeing.'

She adds that swimming can have a meditative effect on the mind. Swimming lengths can at first seem boring, but the repetitive nature of the task allows you to focus on your movement, your body and brings you into the moment, creating a moving meditation. 'In this way swimming can reduce stress and allow minds to calm,' Rebecca says. 'A calm mind has space to learn, be happy and make friends.'

Boost brain power

Tim Hutton, an instructor at swim school Swimming Nature, goes even further in highlighting the benefits of swimming. 'Swimming allows you to shut out the rest of the world and switch off social media for a period of time in a safe and structured environment. Studies have shown that those who take part in sport and exercise regularly achieve higher exam results on average than those who don't.'

Build confidence

Because swimming and the idea of moving with ease through water is a real skill, Tim says that practising and developing it can help on a psychological level too. It's all about honing your self-discipline – learning to rely on and have confidence in your own strength and ability. 'Carrying out sporting endeavours such as swimming to completion can give a real sense of achievement and boost self-esteem and confidence,' he says.

Have fun with friends

Rebecca notes that while swimming is an individual sport, there's a great social aspect to it: 'Swimming can be sociable, it can be fun and that's exactly what is needed to let go of the stresses and expectations of the outside world. When having fun with friends, the focus is on the here and now, and combining this with the calming effects of the water and the sensory stimulation of the activity, you can really let go.'

Swimming allows you to find a peaceful headspace and improve your health and wellbeing at the same time. So, as Tim says: 'Don't count the laps, make the laps count.'

HOW TO BE A SUPER SWIMMER

Just swimming up and down the pool can get boring. Try mixing things up instead with this guide to getting the best from your swim time:

1 Endurance

Focus on developing your ability to swim long distances with minimal rest. Swim for as long as you can continuously followed by a short rest. This will help your body to recover at a quicker rate and you should feel your stamina improving.

2 Technique

Swimming is not a movement that your body can naturally perform, so it's really helpful to work on your swimming technique. This will make all of the other workouts feel better as your swimming will feel more efficient.

Kicking – most swimming pools will have kickboards available to use. If not, they are a great tool to buy. Make sure you hold on to these with both hands and just work on your legs kicking.

Swimming drills – these involve breaking down your swimming stroke to more specific parts to work on these areas. Why don't you give the following a go:

* **One arm drill** – swim with just one arm, the other should remain by your side. Great for front crawl and backstroke.
* **Finger tip drag** – as your hand recovers out of the water, try to drag your fingers along the surface. This helps to raise your elbow and extends your length before your hand enters the water.
* **Fist closed drill** – try to swim with your fists closed. This forces your kicking and your forearms to work hard. Great for front crawl and backstroke technique.

3 Intervals

This is a chance to work on your swimming speed. Try to swim faster than your usual pace for a short distance, rest, then repeat. It's fun to see what time you take to do each repeat and try to improve this each week.

4 Blended

This should be a mixed workout and could include a range of swimming activities, from changing your strokes every five minutes to using pool floats to focusing on a breathing activity – for example, if you usually breathe every third stroke, try to breathe every fifth.

TOP TIPS

* Before climbing into the water to begin your warm-up, do some arm circles to get your shoulders active.

* Most swimming pools will have a clock that you can check to monitor the time of your laps.

* Make sure you have a water bottle on poolside. In the water, you will not feel like you are sweating but your body will be. Stay hydrated!

* Always have a healthy snack in your kit bag. Swimming workouts can make you feel hungry and it's helpful to refuel with something healthy as soon as you can.

* Invest in good goggles that will not leak. This will help you to enjoy your swimming workouts a lot more.

* If your body and legs are feeling quite low in the water, it's always great to go back to the basic floating position and practise this.

STEP BY STEP

'Walking is man's medicine', so said the ancient Greek physician Hippocrates, often referred to as the Father of Western medicine. And it remains the case today. The benefits are numerous – and they're not just physical, especially if you practise mindful walking

WHAT IS MINDFUL WALKING?

Few people pay attention to their surroundings as they dash around every day – be it to school, sports practice, a friend's house or work. Mindful walking can transform these everyday journeys into complete workouts of all five senses. How? By noticing what's going on around you – without judging it – and becoming aware of the sensations that make an appearance as you move. One way to do this is by focusing on one sense at a time, giving that sense all your attention with every step you take.

How can mindful walking improve health?

1 You become physically stronger
Moving more is great for physical health, and walking regularly can be just as good for you as running. It stimulates your circulation, the heart and lungs get a workout, the muscles become stronger, and your posture improves too. If that wasn't enough, studies show that 30 minutes of walking five times a week can even help you sleep better.

2 You get a brain boost
Taking a break from everyday tasks is like pressing the reset button on the brain. You can return to whatever needs to be done afterwards feeling refreshed and ready to go – even that English project you've been pushing to one side might feel more straightforward after a stroll around the block.

3 You can manage emotions
Focusing on the present moment allows you to step away from situations that may feel as though they're constantly swirling around in your mind, causing you stress or anxiety. This helps you to distance yourself from any unpleasant emotions the situation may be causing and to shift your perspective. It can clear your mind of clutter and restore your sense of focus.

MINDFUL WALKING: ONE STEP AT A TIME

Take a while to focus on each of the senses

* **What can you see**? A pretty tree or interesting shadow?

* **What can you hear**? Chirping birds, buses going by or, on a quiet walk, perhaps the sound of your own breath?

* **What can you feel**? A gentle breeze between your fingers or the sensation of pebbles underfoot?

* **What can you taste**? Roll your tongue around your teeth and concentrate. Can you detect the mint of toothpaste or the last vestiges of a lunchtime snack?

* **What can you smell**? Freshly baked bread, new Tarmac?

Take some time to reflect on your experience, how did it make you feel? Start thinking about your next walk. The beauty of mindful walking is that it can be done anywhere. Plan ahead to make sure it's safe and enjoyable.

* Choose a public area that you're familiar with.

* Let someone know your route and what time you expect to return.

* Take your mobile phone with you – on mute while walking to avoid digital distractions.

* Take care around roads and remain aware of traffic.

* Don't walk in darkness.

* Take a drink with you if it's a particularly warm day.

Make it sociable

Mindful walking is a great way to connect with others. Invite a friend along or make it a family occasion. Share the role of leader, allocating a minute or two to guide the group through each sense. Take it in turns to play back experiences while the rest of the group listens.

'BE HAPPY IN THE MOMENT,
THAT'S ENOUGH'

Mother Teresa

A WALK IN THE CLOUDS

Do you know your cirrus from your cumulus? Have you ever seen a cloud that resembles a galloping horse, a fierce dragon, a love heart or an angel? Perhaps it's time to discover the wonders of cloudspotting...

'ONCE YOU HAVE TASTED THE TASTE
OF SKY, YOU WILL FOREVER LOOK UP'

Leonardo Da Vinci

WHY LOOK AT THE CLOUDS?

You have lived underneath the sky all your life, but how many times have you looked up? Have you noticed the ever-changing colour and shapes of clouds as they pass by? Do you know what kind of weather those clouds bring?

Watching clouds might not seem like an exciting way to spend your time at first, but it's surprisingly awe-inspiring. Clouds, which are made of water or ice, float, morph, expand and evaporate moment by moment and it's fascinating to observe. It's even better if you can identify the type of cloud formations and, as a result, forecast the imminent weather.

Although many people love a blue sky and uninterrupted sunshine, cloud enthusiasts enjoy looking up to see drama, variety and the possibility of something unusual or rare. Clouds inspire, too. If it wasn't for the presence of clouds, there wouldn't be great art by the likes of John Constable or JMW Turner and the poet William Wordsworth wouldn't have written the poem *I Wandered Lonely As A Cloud*.

What's amazing about looking at the sky is that it's an ever-changing canvas. The type, colour and volume of cloud is constantly moving. Sometimes, with a little imagination, you will notice a cloud formation that resembles a face, an animal, a mythical creature or a familiar shape.

Watching the clouds pass by enables you to enjoy the moment while also realising that what you see right now might never be seen again.

HOW CLOUDS FORM

Every cloud is made up of tiny droplets of water and ice that have condensed from sun-warmed invisible water vapour that is around us all the time. As air rises, it cools, and eventually the vapour turns back into water to form clouds. As clouds are warmer and lighter than the surrounding cold air, they seem to float like great ships in the sky. If the droplets in the clouds are heavy enough to be pulled down, the water returns to the ground in the form of rain, hail or snow.

HOW TO STUDY CLOUDS

The best way to look up at the sky is by lying on the ground. Choose a quiet place with a good open view. Lie on a blanket and find a position where you can see the clouds rolling by (to prevent damage to your eyes, make sure you avoid facing and looking at the sun).

Of course you don't have to lie down to look up. You can observe the clouds while waiting for a bus or sitting on a park bench. Some of the most dramatic formations appear on the horizon, which means you don't even have to look above your head.

Cloudspotting is one of those hobbies that's completely free. No technical equipment is required, but a camera is recommended. If you happen to be in the right place at the right time to see a rare cloud formation, you'll be happy that you have a camera to get a snapshot of what you've witnessed. You can also take photographs to create a cloud journal or blog.

Today there's renewed interest in cloudspotting, as the use of smartphones is revolutionising the way people see the sky. Amateur cloudspotters who post their images on websites have even snapped new types of cloud never seen before. So why not put that smartphone to good use and see what inspirational images you can take of the white wisps and puffs above your head – even better, have a go at naming them using our cloudspotter's guide over the page…

THE THREE MAIN CLOUD TYPES

1 **Stratus**. These are low level horizontal layers of grey, flat cloud, usually forming a featureless blanket that often covers the whole sky. Stratus may produce rain, fog or snow (depending upon how warm or cold it is).

2 **Cumulus**. Often described as a heap of fluffy cotton wool, these flat-based puffy clouds are often seen on calm, clear, fine-weather days. They can, with the right conditions, grow into towering thunderstorms.

3 **Cirrus**. Thin, wispy high-altitude clouds, sometimes known as 'mare's tails', cirrus are made of ice crystals and are seen at any time of year. Cirrus usually occur in fair weather, but can sometimes appear ahead of deteriorating conditions.

HAVE YOU SPOTTED A RARE CLOUD?

Lenticular. These stationary clouds are lens or saucer-shaped and resemble UFOs. They often appear near mountains.

Fluctus (Kelvin-Helmholtz wave). Forming on windy days, this cloud looks like a rolling wave breaking over the ocean.

Mackerel sky. These swathes of rippled cirrocumulus clouds resemble fish scales. They are usually seen before a change in the weather.

Cavum (Fallstreak holes). These appear as holes or circular gaps in layers of cirrocumulus or altocumulus cloud, and are caused when a patch of moisture suddenly starts to freeze and fall.

Asperitas. Marked by small divot-like features that create chaotic ripples across the sky, these wavy clouds make you feel like you're looking up at a rough sea.

Murus (wall cloud). These develop beneath the base of a strong cumulonimbus cloud and are known to produce severe thunderstorms and tornadoes.

Cauda (tail cloud). A cauda is a distinctive cloud structure that attaches to the right of a wall cloud. It looks a bit like a dinosaur's tail trailing behind a storm. Caused by air flowing into the storm, its tube-like shape can sometimes be mistaken for a tornado.

FREE FROM FEAR

Everyone feels worried from time to time, but have you ever felt so anxious in a situation that you just wanted to run and get out of there? If the answer is yes, you may have experienced a panic attack. They're more common than many people think, but there are ways you can overcome them

What is anxiety?

Anxiety is a primitive and essential emotion. Also known as the fight-or-flight response, it is the body's reaction to something it sees as a threat. When our prehistoric ancestors were tackling or escaping from a mammoth, it was invaluable as it prepared the body to defend itself – for example, the heart beats faster to pump blood to the muscles, providing energy to run away or fight off danger.

When does it become a problem?

Sometimes when the body senses you are afraid, rather than wait to find out whether there is a real danger, it sets off the fight-or-flight response – occasionally this can be so powerful it triggers a panic attack. Any situation you are excessively worried about – for example, performing in front of others, being away from home or sitting an exam – can trigger a panic attack. Sometimes they develop after distressing events like family break-ups or bereavements, or incidents including house fires and car accidents. They can also come out of the blue. Whenever they develop, panic attacks are frightening. They can begin to affect your behaviour and experiences, especially if you live in fear of one happening or worry that something bad will happen because of an attack.

How does it feel?

Imagine you're out with friends and they decide to go to a funfair. You can't explain why, but you just don't feel like going. A sense of unease follows and begins to increase as you approach the crowded fair. Once there, the noise and lights become overwhelming, you start to sweat, feel sick and shaky and you desperately want – need – to run away. This is just one example. You're also likely to feel out of breath and panicky, and because you don't know what's happening, it can be really scary.

The facts about panic attacks

* Panic attacks are the body's fight-or-flight response kicking in. However, sometimes our body reacts when there is no real danger.
* Panic attacks are harmless, although they can feel uncomfortable or scary.
* Panic attacks are brief (typically lasting only 10 to 15 minutes), although they sometimes feel like they go on forever.
* Others (except those very close to you) usually can't tell that you are having a panic attack.

STEPS TO MANAGE PANIC ATTACKS

Understanding your fear is the first step to conquering it. It's important to know that anxiety is common (and it doesn't mean you're crazy) and that you can overcome it – no matter how out of control it feels…

Face your fears
When it comes to conquering anxiety, facing your fears is the key. Avoiding them may make you feel better in the short term, but only by standing firm will you give yourself a chance to discover that nothing bad is going to happen.

Take it step by step
Start by trying to identify feared situations or places. They could be visiting places alone, entering crowded shops or riding the bus. Begin by putting yourself in the least scary situation, let's say it's the bus, for a short time. If possible, take a friend or relative with you for support. Once you feel able to board and stay on the bus for a short time without experiencing too much anxiety, try to move onto the next step. To do this, slightly increase the time you remain on the vehicle. Go at a pace you feel comfortable with and continue adding time in small steps. If you stick with it, the anxiety will fade. The fear of using a bus or train is one of the most common sources of anxiety. Here are some tips to help you if you're facing your fears on public transport:

* **Distraction**. Listening to music or reading a book or magazine can help take your mind off where you are.

* **Google Maps**. Just the simple action of watching the blue dot showing where you're travelling can be a comfort.

* **Mindfulness**. Concentrate on your breathing or look out of the window and take in the landscape around you.

* **Preparation**. Work out beforehand which bus or train you need to catch and the stop where you're getting off.

IF YOU START TO FEEL OVERWHELMED...

It's natural to be anxious as you face your fear, but if you start to feel overwhelmed, stop what you are doing and try to practise a breathing exercise like the one here:

1 Calm breathing
People tend to breathe faster when they're anxious. This can make them dizzy and lightheaded, which often increases feelings of anxiety. Calm breathing involves taking slow, regular breaths through the nose. If you find yourself breathing quickly during a panic attack, calming the breath can help you to feel better.

Try this:
* Breathe in as slowly, deeply and gently as you can through your nose.
* Breathe out slowly, deeply and gently through your mouth.
* Some people find it helpful to count steadily from one to five on each in-breath and each out-breath.
* Close your eyes and focus on your breathing.
* You should start to feel better in a few minutes.

2 Stamp on the spot
Sounds weird, but it works. March on the spot, stamp your feet, and release those stress hormones.

3 Focus on your senses
For example, taste mint-flavoured sweets, or touch or cuddle something soft.

4 Look around
Try to name five things you can see near you, this can help to distract you and take your thoughts to a calmer place.

AFTER A PANIC ATTACK

Look after yourself. It's important to pay attention to what your body needs after you've had a panic attack. For example, you might need to rest somewhere quietly, to eat or drink something. And don't suffer alone – those close to you need to know what you're going through so they can be supportive when you need it.

If you're experiencing anxiety or panic attacks, there are many experts who can help you to overcome these fears. Talk to someone you trust and see your doctor for advice.

TOO MUCH THINKING?

Reflecting on things can be a great way to gain perspective and learn from experiences. But there's a fine line between contemplation and overthinking. Putting your brain through such overtime isn't always the best thing for happiness and self-confidence and might even lead to excessive worrying, often called 'rumination'

Trigger points

Many things can prompt overthinking, from what to wear to a friend's party to a looming homework deadline. It's easy suddenly to feel stressed by an event that initially didn't seem troublesome. Often that's because there's overthinking going on and the importance of the party or deadline is exaggerated in your mind, causing worry and self-doubt.

It's a habit that affects pretty much everyone at some point, but it can be managed. Firstly, place yourself – and your thoughts – in the here and now. Identifying thoughts that have overthinking potential as soon as you first become aware of them will allow you to apply the brakes and help to ensure they only occupy their appropriate share of energy and headspace.

Rather than let thoughts overwhelm you and affect your self-belief, use the easy guide on the next page to stop overthinking in its tracks. Practise noticing when you're beginning to overthink and try to keep those racing thoughts in check. Remember, you have the power to recognise and control your thoughts before they really get going – just don't overthink it!

WHAT TO DO IF YOUR BRAIN'S WORKING OVERTIME

1 Bring yourself to the present moment
Overthinking works by taking your mind away from what is in front of you in the present moment and instead making you imagine things that are in the future. Bringing yourself back to the present moment when you notice your mind racing can quieten those thoughts. You could become engaged with the present by drawing your attention to something physically near you. For example, the colour of an object, fellow passengers on a bus, the size of a building or the shape of a tree – anything that is happening and exists in the here and now. Taking a moment to focus on something real can halt overthinking and calm the mind.

2 Coming up with your own phrase of calm
As overthinking works by worrying about events that are in the future – and therefore aren't factual – try to counter this with a short memorable phrase that you can pull out when the going gets tough. Something as simple as 'this is not true' can prevent anxious thoughts spiralling. Most worries don't come to pass, so finding your own unique phrase to emphasise this point can help to ground your brain in reality.

3 Get creative
Picking up a pen to do some writing, sketching or colouring will keep your mind occupied and can relieve stress. Alternatively, you may find expressing your worries creatively releases them and also helps to stop overthinking. Either way, there are benefits to be found through engaging the brain in a different and creative way to its usual activity.

'THOUGHTS AREN'T FACTS, SO DON'T TAKE THEM SERIOUSLY'

Ruby Wax

4 Changing your environment or physicality

Sometimes it won't be possible to get up and leave the room in which you find yourself overthinking, but if you are able to change your environment, it can be a good idea. Moving to a different room in the same building, or even going outside for some fresh air, can give the brain pause as the physical act of moving will provide a change of focus, even if it's just on how to get to your new destination. If it isn't possible to move location, try changing your posture – often people become hunched over when they're stressed. Relaxing your shoulders and sitting straight will make your posture feel more energised and confident.

5 Breathe deeply

Monitoring your breathing is another way to bring the attention back to your body. Taking deep breaths and focusing on how many seconds you wish to draw out the breath (try counting to four beats per breath inwards and outwards) can help to distract from racing thoughts.

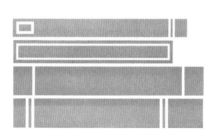

WAKE UP
AND STRETCH

Why the ancient art of yoga is the ideal way to begin
your day and how it's never too soon to get started

Yoga is the harmonisation of the mind, body and soul. It is an art form that's many thousands of years old – cave drawings show that yoga was practised more than 5,000 years ago. Its main root is in India, but yoga images have also been depicted in ancient Egypt, China and South America.

It is thought that thousands of years ago ancient yogis observed the world around them, its interconnection and flow, and from these observations yoga sprung forth.

YOGA COVERS SEVERAL LIMBS, OR BRANCHES, OF TEACHING

There are two main limbs:
The first are called **asanas** – these are a series of rhythmic and graceful movements of various joints and muscles of the body aimed at achieving particular postures and the physical conditioning of the body that goes along with them.

The second is called **Pranayama** – this is a Sanskrit word (coming from the classical language of India) and means lifeforce or breath control. This involves breathing activities to produce specific results.

The breath is vital for a healthy body. Look at these numbers:
On average, a healthy body can survive… *3 weeks without food, 3 days without water, 3 minutes without breathing.*

Practising yoga regularly has been proven to provide many health benefits. Based on the premise that everything is energy, yoga supports a healthy body by working on its different points and lines to maintain a healthy flow of energy, circulatory system and immune system.

So why not get in the yoga mood with our easy guide (overleaf) to one of the most common asanas, the Sun Salutation.

SALUTE TO THE SUN

Referred to as the Sun Salutation (its Sanskrit name is *Surya Namaskar*), this is a wonderful yoga activity that balances and energises the body. Have fun practising it in the morning when you wake up and see how it invigorates you for your day.

1 Stand tall, holding your hands, palms together, in prayer pose at your heart's centre. Take a few deep breaths and focus on the self, your core, your inner sun.

2 Breathing in, circle your hands above your head, reaching tall to the sun. Look up to the sky through open arms.

3 On an out breath, flow your arms down in a circle around your body to rest on the outside of each foot, with your fingers pointing forward in line with your toes. If needed, bend your knees slightly. Let your head hang forward like a rag doll.

4 On an in breath, lift your head, look forward and step your left foot back into a lunge.

5 On an out breath, step your right foot back to join your left, forming a straight line with your body, known as plank pose.

6 On an out breath, bend your knees and lower your body. Keep your knees on the floor and your elbows tucked in near the body.

7 Breathing in, push your chest upward into Cobra pose (*Bhujangasana*), opening your chest by drawing your shoulders back – take a few breaths here.

8 On an out breath, tuck your toes under and push up into Downward Dog position, pushing down into the floor through your hands and feet while your hips pull upward.

9 On an in breath, look up and step your right foot forward between your hands, forming a lunge position.

10 Gently bring your left foot forward to join the right one, forming a forward fold with your body.

11 Breathing in, slowly circle your hands up around your body, and lift yourself to a standing tall position (your head comes up last). The hands join above the head in prayer position.

12 Lower the hands to prayer pose at your heart's centre and take a few deep breaths. Then repeat the sequence, this time starting with taking the right leg back first at the beginning lunge pose.

Declutter
YOUR BEDROOM

Have you tidied your bedroom lately? You're probably thinking you have better things to do, but a few minutes each day will go a long way to making your private space a great place to be

Your bedroom is your personal space, a safe haven where you can be yourself, relax, learn, daydream and sleep. It's also a space where you keep everything you own and that might include stuff accumulated over many years. If you walk into your room and think, 'there's a bed in there somewhere', and you can't remember what your floor looks like, it's probably a sign you need to declutter.

Sifting through everything you have and deciding what you need to keep, bin, recycle or give away sounds like a chore, but it's easier than you think and there are plenty of advantages. When you clear out the things you no longer need, you create more space and improve the energy in your room. Having less stuff will make it simple to find what you do have, and tidying your room will take less effort.

So, how do you declutter your room (particularly if it's the messiest it's ever been) and, more importantly, ensure it stays tidy?

If you're feeling overwhelmed by the task, focus on clearing and cleaning one drawer, box or corner of the room at a time and work your way round. You don't have to do it all in one go. Decluttering can be tiring and intense, particularly on an emotional level. Do a little every day. Take your time, especially when it comes to deciding whether you need to keep sentimental items or not. Letting go of things you no longer need is refreshing and worth the effort. Once your room is clean and free of clutter, it will feel fresh, cosy and inviting.

TIPS FOR A CLUTTER-FREE ROOM

* Designate a place for everything you have so that it's easy to find. Use a keepsake box for precious things; box files for homework and notes; storage boxes for games or sports equipment; shelves for books; drawers and wardrobe for storing clean clothes; and a laundry bag for your washing.

* Have a small bin near your bedroom door and instantly dispose of whatever can't be reused.

* Do you have a drawer full of electronic gadgets, earphones, cables and chargers? Look through them and let go of what you no longer use.

* Go through your stuff and declutter every few months. You'll be surprised by what you accumulate in such a short time and the clothes you've outgrown or that you no longer wear.

* Wherever you can, recycle or gift anything you no longer need. It's better for you and the environment.

* Try to keep a decluttering box ready at all times. Put it somewhere you can't miss it and get rid of it as soon as it's full. Aim to put a few things in it each day and you will start to see a difference soon.

* And remember. Don't let anyone talk you into getting rid of something if you're not sure. It's okay to have stuff as long as it makes you happy. You're the best judge of that.

STAY OR GO?

If you can't decide whether to keep, bin, recycle or donate an item to charity, ask yourself these questions:

* What am I saving it for?
* Do I need it?
* Do I actually like it?
* Is it something I still use?
* When am I likely to use it again?
* Does it still fit?
* When did I last wear it?
* Is it broken?
* Can it be repaired?
* How does it make me feel?

* Does it have any sentimental value?
* Why do I feel attached to it?
* Will I miss it if I let it go?
* Does it remind me of good or bad times?
* Do I really need seven (or whatever the number) of these?
* Can I recycle it or give it to someone who needs it more?

SUCCULENTS
for starters

An indoor windowsill is the perfect spot to grow some succulent plants. Why succulents? With just a bit of care and attention, they'll thrive – they'll even withstand some neglect. Plus they come in a range of sizes, shapes and colours, offering plenty of scope to relax and unwind as you put together creative displays

WHAT ARE SUCCULENTS?

They're plants that have naturally evolved to survive droughts and are often found in deserts, rocky outcrops and coastal areas. In all, there are some 10,000 species worldwide. They need light and water to grow – after all, they are living things – but because they store water in their leaves they don't need watering as often as most plants. The thickened leaves tend to be full and fleshy, often with a waxy coating to help keep in moisture, which can make them look white, silver or mauve. Cacti are also succulents, but they tend to have sharp spines or prickly hairs, making them trickier to handle and arrange in patterns.

SOME LESS PRICKLY SUCCULENTS INCLUDE:

Aloe vera. You may already have heard of this one as it's an ingredient in many skin cosmetics. The plant has long, tongue-like leaves that if cut through release a sticky gel that soothes burned or sore skin. Aloe vera makes a good, medium-sized pot plant for a kitchen windowsill and is handy for treating minor cooking burns quickly – simply cut off a leaf and apply the cut surface to the skin.

Jade plant or **money tree** (*Crassula ovata*). This is associated with good fortune and friendship in Chinese culture. The plant is used in the practice of feng shui (placing objects in particular places in the home to create a more harmonious environment). Jade plants can last for years and grow into beautiful shapes like miniature indoor trees – you sometimes see them in Chinese restaurants.

Low-growing succulents. Small, round or fist-shapes such as **Mexican snowball** (*Echeveria elegans*) and **zebra cactus** (*Haworthia*) are often sold unnamed. Just pick out a group of similar sizes looking for a contrast of colour, patterns and leaf shape. You can rearrange them all together in a shallow container, when viewed from above this gives either a carpet effect or grid in a square container. Single plants can be planted in a rock or shell if you have nimble fingers.

BUYING TIPS

* Look for succulents in houseplant sections of garden centres, supermarkets or florists. Artificial succulents may look realistic but are made of plastic so be sure to get living plants. These will have soil in the pots.

* Aloe vera and jade plant are sold as single pot plants already in a plastic plant pot with holes. To put them on a windowsill you'll also need a pot cover (without holes) or a saucer.

* Smaller succulents, which could be the size of a thumb right up to fist size, are often sold in a mix-and-match style so you can select the ones you want.

* Leaves should feel firm and fleshy, not floppy or damaged. If the base of the stem near the soil feels very wet or rotten then don't buy the plant as the roots will have been damaged by too much water.

* If you want to display a collection of succulents in another bigger pot then also buy houseplant compost (cactus compost is the most suitable for succulents) and a small bag of grit or perlite (white granules). Find out what to do on the next page.

CARING FOR LIVING PLANTS

Once your plants are in your chosen containers, find somewhere indoors that gets plenty of natural sunlight but is frost-free.

Let the compost (soil) dry out between watering. Push your finger into the soil and if it feels dry give the plant some water. Usually water once a week or once a fortnight depending on whether the plant is actively growing. You can put a pot with holes into a saucer of water for 20-30 minutes then remove it, this is called watering from below, but don't leave the pot standing in water because even after only an hour the roots can be damaged. You can also water directly onto the compost from above, but avoid the leaves.

Succulents grow slowly but if they thrive they may produce little babies around the edge of the parent plant. You can remove these carefully with a small knife and pot them into their own small pots of compost – with luck these might grow on and you can expand your collection or give some as gifts to friends and family.

If you care for an aloe vera or jade plant really well they might get too big for the windowsill and begin to fall over. You can cut off some of the larger branches or leaves to stabilise them or move the plant on to a bigger pot.

It is straightforward to put plants into different or bigger pots but it can make a mess, so use a flat surface covered with a tray or newspaper. Tilt the pots up and ease the plants out, being gentle with the roots. Half-fill the new pot with compost, break it up with your fingers and then press it down lightly. Position the plant in its new pot, fill compost around it and press it in gently. When the roots are covered, a finishing touch is to put a shallow layer of grit or similar over the surface of the compost.

'ALL GOOD THINGS ARE WILD AND FREE'

Henry David Thoreau

THE POWER OF SILENCE

While we might think we know what silence is, in a world of stress, technology and digital chatter, finding it can be a challenge

Noise is everywhere, and it's almost inescapable. You leave the chatter of the classroom for a relaxing lunch and you're met by another cacophony of sounds – plates clattering, doors closing, cutlery banging… There's construction on the street, traffic zooming, music blaring. At home phones bleep, the washing machine whirrs, the television's on, your sister's playing the piano. Somehow, you never quite feel rested. Yet practising a few minutes of silent reflection every day can improve your health.

WHY SILENCE IS GOLDEN

* Silence helps create harmony within. Removing noise gives you time to think, which can lead to a more balanced sense of wellbeing.

* Silence could have a big effect on your health. A 2013 study of the effect of noise on mice found that just two hours of silence a day led to the development of new brain cells in the hippocampus, the area of the brain responsible for learning, memory and emotion.

* Silence has long been a feature of world religions and many religious orders still practise it to find a higher spiritual understanding.

* Loud noises raise stress levels by activating the brain's amygdala and causing the release of the stress hormone cortisol.

* Just as too much noise can cause stress and tension, research has found that silence has the opposite effect, releasing tension in the brain and body. A study in the journal *Heart* found two minutes of silence to be more relaxing than listening to soothing music, based on changes in blood pressure and blood circulation in the brain.

STEPS TO A NOISE DETOX

1 Disconnect
Turn off everything – your phone, computer and television. Anything that hums or beeps or rings. If you can't safely turn it off, then mute it instead.

2 Give yourself some space
Encourage your family to take off on a trip without you. Solitude is a powerful aid to silence. Being on your own gives your brain a rest from constant distractions.

3 Daydream or mind travel
Silence gives your mind clarity and without any disruptions you can think far more deeply. Use it to go have an adventure, or else solve a problem that has been bugging you. You will find that silence helps you concentrate far more effectively.

4 Be thankful for who you are and what you have
By giving yourself this time of quiet reflection, you can focus on the positive elements of your life. You will gain a greater appreciation of who you are and what makes your life special, particularly the relationships you have with other people.

5 Concentrate your mind
What sounds can you hear? A chorus of birdsong? Insects? The wind sweeping through trees? Someone walking on gravel? You might find that you end up hearing more by learning to embrace silence.

'SILENCE IS THE SLEEP THAT NOURISHES WISDOM'

Francis Bacon

HOW TO DO A
DIY RETREAT

What's the solution when you need a relaxing break from
everyday life but can't get away? Learn how to create your own
feel-good experience at home

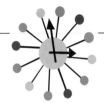

YOUR PAMPER PLAN

1 The week before
Decide when you are going to set up your DIY retreat. Choose a day or two when you don't have to study, work or go out. Let your friends know you won't be contactable on social media and tell your family you plan to take some time to boost your wellbeing. Consider what you will do, too. What activities will you try? Walking in peaceful surroundings is easy to organise, but you may have to carry out research in advance for other activities, such as meditation or yoga.

2 Two days before
Stock up on fruit, veg and water, enough to see you through the duration of your retreat, and consider what other food might be necessary. While you will want to be healthy to help you recharge, you don't want to feel miserable or hungry. This retreat is a physical as well as a spiritual reboot. Your body will thank you for it.

3 The day before
Ensure any outstanding chores, homework and messages are completed. You will want to concentrate all your energies on restoring your inner-balance, not worrying about whether you've responded to WhatsApp messages. Also, you could change your bed sheets – there's nothing quite like getting into freshly laundered linen to induce the most delicious sense of calm for the beginning of your retreat.

4 The night before
Is anything stressing you out? Write any problems on a sheet of paper and then put your list in a drawer. Make a vow not to fret about these things for the duration of your retreat. You might want to select some books to read. Also think about how you're going to spend your day so that you allow time for thinking, exercise or relaxation.

YOUR DIY RETREAT

To begin your retreat, turn off the television and anything that rings, bells or beeps. Do not be tempted to look at your social media or what's happening in the world at large as it will distract you from this precious downtime. Make yourself a healthy breakfast or prepare the meals you've decided upon. Try not to have anything that contains caffeine. Drink lots of water throughout your retreat. You have the luxury of the whole day ahead with no interruptions and, if you have a timetable to follow, all well and good.

For those who prefer to go with the flow and see how they feel on the day,
here are a few ideas…

1 **Try meditating**. You may already know how to do this, if not you could use one of the countless free apps available (okay, so you have to use a phone for this, but if you are a beginner, you may well find an app helpful). Alternatively, you could try our awareness meditation (see page 32) and yoga exercise (page 100).

2 **Try silence**. This may be easy or not, depending on where you live. If you are in a city with its background hum of horns, sirens and train rumblings, put on noise-cancelling headphones.

3 **Water therapy**. Recreate the feeling of being in a spa in your own bathroom. If whoever owns your home doesn't mind, light some naturally scented candles, give yourself a salt scrub, then relax under a long shower or in a hot bath (be careful not to scald yourself, though). In this way you're helping to rejuvenate your body as well as your mind. You'll also smell gorgeous afterwards.

4 **Listen to nature**. You may live deep in the countryside or by the coast but if you don't, there are plenty of apps to make you feel as if you do, such as the free app Forest Sounds, which will help transport you to a different place, soothe away anxieties or send you off to sleep.

5 **Step outside**. It is one thing to listen to nature, even better to get out in it if you can. Find a green space where you can appreciate the beauty of the natural world. The more you can stop your mind wandering and thinking about your everyday life and work, the more energised you will feel.

After your retreat is over, you may want to go back to the drawer with your list of anxieties. Is it still as worrying as you first thought? Perhaps your relaxation time brought you some perspective? Solutions may well have presented themselves, or at least you will now feel more energised to tackle whatever was bothering you.

ONLY AN HOUR TO SPARE?

If you can, get out into some green space and take time to look at all nature has to offer. Practise your breathing in a park or walk around a garden and really look at nature's exquisite handiwork wherever you can find it. Feel your breathing slow, try to clear your head of any issues and take joy in the moment of peace.

The art of
TAKING A BATH

The art of taking... a bath? Really? Yes, taking a bath doesn't have to be just about getting clean. Do it with care and attention and it can become one of life's simple pleasures...

BATH INSTRUCTIONS

Who needs instructions to take a bath? Well, it may be obvious, but it's also easy to forget that some simple planning can turn bathing time into a great pampering experience…

Choose the right moment so you don't have to rush, ideally in the evening.

Unless you're using it to play music, turn off your phone. Either lock the door or hang up a 'Do not disturb' sign (whichever's allowed at home) so you're not interrupted.

Get a small washcloth to cushion your neck and gather all the products you will need.

Make sure to have a good book or magazine to read.

If you have a safe place to position a phone or device, put on some relaxing music.

Light one or two candles with extra care (ask permission if needed), or consider LED lights for a similar effect.

Place towels on the radiator so you stay warm when you get out.

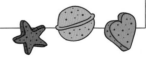

PAMPER YOURSELF...

When the bath is full and the water is a comfortable temperature (it should be hot but not scalding), ease yourself slowly in and indulge all your senses – you deserve it…

* Use essential oils to nourish the skin.
* Enjoy a good body scrub with a natural fibre brush.
* Apply a face mask to clear pores.
* Finish with a hair mask for extra moisture and shine.

BATH MEDITATION

This relaxation technique involves breathing slowly and fully as well as concentrating on the sounds and sensations of the water:

Lie down and lower the back of your head into the water (unless you have a face or hair mask on). Your face should remain above the surface so you can breathe easily through your nose and mouth.

Now tilt your head slightly back, just so your ears are under the water. It's easier to focus on your breathing when external sounds are blocked out.

Place one hand on your stomach and the other on your chest and breathe in through your nose and out through your mouth. Let your breathing become slower and deeper and feel each of your hands rising in turn as you inhale and exhale.

Focus your attention on all of these sensations, from the warmth of the water on your skin to the movement of your hands, to the sound of your breathing. Within no time, you'll be floating in a state of calm. Remember, though, the idea is to be aware of the calmness, so you need to remain fully awake.

BATH BENEFITS

Do you know the healing powers of a long, hot soak?

Detox and cleanse
Sweating is your body's natural way of detoxifying: hot water opens the pores causing you to sweat and release toxins, which results in fresher and cleaner skin.

Reduce cold symptoms
Similarly, the heat opens the nasal passages and relieves congestion by reducing inflammation. The steam created clears sinuses and chest, helping you to breathe more easily.

Calm pains
Adding sea salts or Epsom salts to your bath will help to relax tight muscles and loosen stiff joints. They also calm the central nervous system and can help to reduce headaches.

Relieve skin conditions
Baking soda acts as a mild antiseptic for itchy and dry skin conditions. Adding some to your bath can help to leave skin clean and smooth and minimise irritability.

Reduce stress
The deep state of relaxation you feel is created by the sense of weightlessness and the massaging-like sensation of the water.

Help to sleep
A relaxing bath will reduce brain activity while the gradual drop in body temperature that one experiences after a bath can help you fall asleep more quickly.

Top tips for a
GOOD NIGHT'S SLEEP

Make sure your bedroom is cool, dark and quiet – there shouldn't be any noise to disturb your sleep. Consider introducing soothing scents to help you to relax.

Try to go to bed at about the same time every night so your body and mind know when to get ready to slow down.

Avoid heavy meals in the evening as a full stomach can be uncomfortable and disrupt your sleeping patterns.

Have a relaxing bedtime routine and avoid activities that keep the mind whirring, like watching TV, using a phone or playing video games.

A bath is a great way to unwind both mind and body.

If you're a worrier, try writing to-do lists for the next day. Once your tasks are on paper – or in your phone – they'll be less likely to cloud your mind and keep you awake.

Exercising during the day will help and simple breathing exercises (check out our Belly Breath meditation on page 32) just before going to bed are also useful.

Still can't sleep? Don't worry. Just try to keep your thoughts positive and concentrate on one or two things that brought you happiness or reassurance during the day.

TEEN Breathe

TEEN BREATHE is a trademark of Guild of Master Craftsman Publications Ltd

First published 2019 by Ammonite Press
an imprint of Guild of Master Craftsman Publications Ltd
Castle Place, 166 High Street, Lewes, East Sussex, BN7 1XU, United Kingdom

www.ammonitepress.com
www.teenbreathe.co.uk

Editorial: Susie Duff, Catherine Kielthy, Jane Roe

Publisher: Jonathan Grogan

Words and diet: Dawattie Basdeo, Vicky H Bourne, Jim Butler, Jenny Cockle, Tracy Darnton,
Liz Dobbs, Edward Field, Donna Findlay, Jade Angeles Fitton, Anne Guillot, Tracy Hallett,
Catherine Kielthy, Sarah Maynard, Tanyel Mustafa, Kate Orson, Victoria Pickett, Sarah Rodrigues,
Sarah Rudell Beach, Simone Scott, Carol Anne Strange, Renee van der Vloodt

Illustrations: Shutterstock.com, Anieszka Banks, Fern Choonet, Claire van Heukelom,
Ginnie Hsu, Samantha Nickerson, Emily Portnoi, Sara Thielker, Céleste Wallaert

Cover illustration: Charly Clements

ISBN 978 1 78145 475 6

A catalogue record for this book is available from the British Library

Colour reproduction by GMC Reprographics
Printed and bound in Turkey

AMMONITE
PRESS